Fight the Fear

by James Summers

Copyright © 2019 James Summers

The rights of James Summers to be identified as the author of this work have been asserted in accordance with the Copyright, Designs and Patents Act 1988. All rights reserved.

Except for the quotation of small passages for the purposes of criticism and review, no part of this publication may be reproduced, stored in a retrieval system, or transmitted, in any form or by any means, electronic, mechanical, photo copying, recording or otherwise, except under the terms of the Copyright, Designs and Patents Act 1988, and without the prior consent of the publisher.

Too Many Have Died.
Too Many Lives Have Been Destroyed.
Stop Government Child Abuse Cover Ups.
It's Time For The Truth…

I'm James Summers and this is my story. It's about my life in care and the horrific experiences I've lived through.

I've had to deal with bullies. The loss of family, and friends that I never saw again. I've seen deaths from drugs…the lost ones who took the wrong path and were robbed of their childhoods.

If you look around your hometown, how many kids do you imagine have run away from abuse they've suffered in a care home? I can only tell you what I know to be fact, in the hope my book might help someone out there. I feel I have to do this to help me with my own feelings, and to show my family that there's more to me than they think.

I want people to know what I had to deal with as a young boy when I was put in care, and to show the whole world that changes must be made. The system is broken.

Chapter One

As children in care, myself and those around me were bullied, kicked, punched and locked in rooms for days on end. We were given no food and were made to stand on cold floors in just our underwear and a vest.

I remember one night being pulled out of bed; a hand was placed over my mouth and I was dragged to a dark room and battered for no reason.

I was pushed from one care home to another, which meant my abusers were never caught. From the age of seven I went through some really really dark times. I felt sad and lonely as I had no one to talk to about the abuse. The longer it went on the more I ran away, getting into shit. The police never listened, they just took me back to the abusers where I was battered again.

*

My first kids' home was a place called Grove House in Liverpool. I think I was about six, maybe seven, at the time. At first, people said, "Hi, are you okay?" and all that shit, but after a few days had gone by the slaps started. Then the punches and kicks.

I was locked in my room and starved. I was bullied, poked, and was slapped across the face by a man who was ten times bigger than me. I could tell he enjoyed it.

The first open window I saw, I was gone. Free. I ran like a madman. In my mind, there was no chance he would catch me. I was on the run for days and days. I'd walk along the Leeds-Liverpool canal, on my own, aged seven. I remember thinking to myself, "I'm a free boy! No more slaps, no more pokes, no more kicks."

My freedom was cut short when a big, fat policeman, who had a photo of me on his dashboard, spotted me. "Get in," he said, "you're going back to Grove House."

I tried to tell him what had happened to me when I'd been in there, but he didn't listen to me. I was crying my eyes out as I explained how I'd been beaten up and made to do things that were sick and evil. How they picked on me every day and night and how I was made to eat food I didn't like. I was so scared to even get out my bed to use the toilet that I wet my bed every night. The next morning they'd batter me for it and call me a 'dirty boy'.

There was one man working there who used to drag me out of bed by my hair. He'd make me stand in the corner in the dark for hours and call me fat.

I told this policeman everything. He still said he was taking me back. "You're staying there," he sneered. "You're telling lies. Don't be running off again."

Though I was only seven, I can remember feeling so fucking angry that he was taking me back.

Throughout the drive back to Grove House I looked for a way out, but the doors had child locks on them. I sat in the back, shitting myself and screaming, terrified about what they would do to me on my return.

"Please, please don't take me back," I begged. "They'll kill me. They'll hit me and lock me in my room for days."

That's what I had to deal with as a young child. I had no idea then that it was only the start of things to come.

*

My first care home was nasty. There were other kids there at the same time as me, but I cannot speak about them and what happened. I feel I have the right to talk about myself; it's my life and I'll do as I please with it. This is what I feel I must do. I might become side-tracked but writing this is stressful.

Back at the shithole that was Grove House, this big, fat man stood on the doorstep; he was massive to me, aged seven. "Right, you, get in there!" He slapped me across the face and pushed me into a door. He then dragged me into his office.

"Get off me, you fat cunt," I screamed, spitting at him.

He put his hand over my mouth and punched me in my back. "You'll not run away from me again," he said.

I stopped screaming to shout, "You want to bet, you fucking knobhead! Watch me. Soon as I get the chance, I'm off."

That's what I did. I ran away again and again.

Chapter Two

Some members of staff there were okay, though not many. One called Janet was lovely, she tried to arrange home leave so I could visit my mum, not that this was any better.

My mother was just nasty. She'd say to the staff, "Oh, yes, he can come home at Christmas, as long as he's good in there and does as he's told."

Janet explained the deal. "Look, Jimmy, don't run away and, please, just listen to us, and you'll get to go home for a little while."

"Fine," I said. I vowed to listen and get through the next few months by being a good little boy, rather than putting my energies into my next runaway plan.

The day came when I was due to go home. Then came the call from my mother. "Sorry, Jimmy can't come home this Christmas," she'd told the staff.

Whilst she was on the phone, I was sat on the doorstep of the kids' home with my backpack on, waiting. I was the only kid there, but I was happy. "It's the first time in three years I'm going home for Christmas," I thought.

The big, fat man came. "Listen, Jimmy," he said, "you'll have to stay here for Christmas. Your mother has rung and said you can't go home for the holidays."

My head popped and that was it. I was off, running down the lane with my backpack, thinking, "You fucking bitch! How could you do this to me, the only kid left in that home for Christmas?"

I made my way to my hometown by walking along the Leeds-Liverpool canal path. As I walked, I thought about what I was going to say to my mother about her phone call. I reached her house and hid on the other side of the wall. I didn't knock in case the home had told her what had happened and she'd called the police. For all I knew, they could have been in there already, waiting for me.

Hours went by. It was cold and I was hungry. I could see the Christmas tree lights twinkling through the window and I just cried my eyes out. "Why me?"

I climbed over the wall and sneaked up to the window. I looked for any sign of the police but there was none.

I knocked and she opened the door. "Why are you here?" she snapped. "I don't want you here."

"I've run away."

"You can't come in," she said, and closed the door on me. I wasn't to know this, but she immediately phoned the police to tell them I'd turned up at her door.

I was devastated. "What a bitch. Doing that to her son on Christmas eve."

The police came and picked me up. They took me straight back to Grove

House. "You've got to stop running away, Jimmy," they said.

"No." I said, "As soon as you take me back there, I'll do it again, but this time I'll not come to my mother's, I'll run miles and miles away, where you'll never find me. Then you can't bring me back to where they bully me."

The police took no notice. They never listened to what I said and just took me back there every time I ran off.

Whenever I was returned the same shit would happen. I'd be stripped to my underwear and made to stand in a cold corner of the kitchen all night long.

Chapter Three

This went on and on for about two years. It was the same shit every week…slaps, kicks, punches, being told I was a bad boy and that my mother didn't want me, which is why she'd dumped me there. No wonder I ran off whenever I saw the opportunity.

I remember one big, fat man, called Gary. When he tried to get in my face, I said, "Fuck off! You're not my dad. I can do what I please."

That just made him angry. He pinned me to the floor and twisted my arms behind my back like a chicken.

Other members of staff joined in. What they thought was fun was abuse at the highest level.

They left no marks. No bruising. Instead, they starved me, and I was made to stand in corners for hours on end.

*

After the episode with my mum and being shunned at Christmas, and once all the other kids had come back from their home visits, I began planning my escape yet again.

My key worker had been warned that if I ran away again, I wouldn't be allowed to come back to Grove House once caught. "You'll end up somewhere else, you know."

"I don't care," I said. "Fuck you all. I'll do what I like, just like you lot do to me."

It wasn't long before I was walking along the Leeds-Liverpool canal again, still only eight years of age.

There was no sign of my mother.

My dad was a hard worker who loved his drink. I'm not going to disparage him; in my eyes, he tried. My mother would say things she wouldn't keep to, like home leave. She'd sit with her friends and talk about 'how bad her son Jimmy was'.

What a cow. She should have tried harder.

*

That was what happened during my time at Grove House: I constantly ran away or fought with the staff and the other kids. I hated it there. In the end I was removed after smashing the place up.

I was taken to a place called Sterrix Lane in Litherland. During the night they just came and got me; they didn't say anything about where we were going, they just told me to get in the car.

It was a short trip; we remained in Liverpool. "Not too bad, then," I thought. It was still dark outside when we pulled up. The building looked old and crumbling.

I got out of the car. "What's this shithole? You think I'm staying here?"

The member of staff accompanying me said, "You'll never run away from here, Jimmy." They had a huge smirk across their face. "Your mother doesn't want you, that's why we have to put up with you, you little bastard. Now get in there."

"Knobhead," I spat.

I walked towards the doorway and out came this big bloke with massive eyes popping out of his face. "Hello, Jimmy," he said, "I'm John. I'm your master."

"Like fuck you are. I'm only eight."

"Follow me to your room, Jimmy. You'll be happier here, son."

"You're not my dad, don't call me son," I snapped.

We walked down a hallway. A kid was walking the opposite way. "Alright, Jimmy lad! Why you here?"

I smiled. It was an old friend from one of the kids' home I'd been in. "Yes," I thought, "Let's make plans…"

"I'll see you after," I said.

As I began to settle into this new home there was a knock on my bedroom door. It was him, the big fat head. He popped his head round the door. "Can you come to my office, Jimmy? We need to talk about your stay here."

As I got up to follow him, he pushed me back onto the bed. "Listen, you little shithead, if you ever run away from here or give any of my staff a hard time, I'll slap your face silly." He whacked me right across the face.

That's how it was every time he was on duty. I spent most of my time trying to stop being pinned down by them. I still ran away, so nothing really changed.

If they locked me in my room, I'd smash a window and run off. But I'd always get picked up by the police.

I spent two years there.

One day I was watching television with an older girl, just chilling out, when John Fathead came. "Jimmy, you have a visitor."

"I don't get visitors," I said. "Why lie, knobhead?"

"Talk to me like that and I'll tell him to go."

I sighed but went downstairs to the visiting area, where I caught sight of my visitor. It was my older brother. "Fuck," I muttered to myself.

"Look, I've just come to say, please just stay here and stop running off," he said.

I shook my head. "It's not happening. Soon as I get the chance, I'm out of here. You see that big, fat knobhead?" I pointed to John. "He slapped me across the face and stood on my back. You think I'm staying here? You're joking, right?"

My brother turned and left.

Once he'd gone, Fathead said, "Right, get upstairs now."

"Fuck off, you fat knobhead!" I shouted. "You're just a bully."

He chased me round the tables, but he didn't catch me. The other kids watched as he eventually cornered me. He dragged me by my neck around the corner to the bottom of the stairs then punched me in the face.

"What a fucking bully!" I was so mad. "You're dead, you fat prick," I screamed.

He pinned me to the stairs, but I managed to squirm free. I gave him the best kick to the balls you've ever heard of, despite the fact I was just eight years old and fighting off a fully-grown man.

He took a step back. I took advantage of my position on the steps and kicked him in the head, then I ran like fuck to get to my room. Once there, I smashed the window to get out onto the roof.

"I'll get you, you little bastard!" he screamed.

"Come on then," I said. I pulled slate from the roof and started throwing it down at him. I was so angry, I felt there was no turning back.

I could see the staff running around the grounds, staring up at me. "Come on, you fucking dickheads!"

"Get down!" someone shouted. "The police will be here soon."

"Bring the police." I shouted back.

After I'd been on the roof for half an hour the police came and dragged me into Fathead's office. The police stood there and said nothing as he poked me in the face.

"Is he getting charged for this?" said one of the officers, nodding at me.

"No," said Fathead. "I'll deal with him."

The police left and he dragged me to my room, locking me in. I spent the night crying to myself. Morning came and another staff member unlocked the door. "Come with me, please. We need to talk about your stay here and the way you've been."

I got up and followed him to his office. As I walked through the door I was slapped and pushed into the corner. Punches rained down on my back and my belly until I was on the floor. They straddled me.

"Get off me, you fucking cunts!" I screamed. "Get off me now!" The only thing I could do was bite. I clamped down hard on his calf so he'd let go of me.

"That's assault!" he screamed at me.

"Yeah, and what about all the times you've hit me, you fat piece of shit!"

"You're getting removed from here, to a place called Saint Vincent's in Formby. It's just for boys like you."

Chapter Four

It's difficult to remember exactly how old I was, specific dates, or what year I stayed at certain places off the top of my head…though I do have this information in my files.

I believe I was roughly ten years of age when I was moved to Saint Vincent's. It was a strange looking place. Evil, even. I could feel the horrible atmosphere before we got to the main door. I was shitting myself. Wide-eyed, I looked around me, clocking the routes out of there, should I have needed them.

I didn't like the place one bit. It was dark and dingy and there was no sign of life. No kids looking out of windows, nothing. I had such a strange feeling within me.

The car stopped and a man opened my door. "Get out, you're here," he said. "Welcome to Saint Vincent's. Follow me."

Another member of staff held my arm. We walked, the man talked. I didn't listen.

I scanned the place for other kids but there wasn't one in sight. "Am I the only one in this place?" I thought.

We entered a big hallway that had huge rooms leading from it, which looked like offices. The wooden flooring and décor made Saint Vincent's look as dark and foreboding inside as it did on the outside. It might as well have had 'Welcome to Hell' written on the door.

The man asked me to follow him as he entered one of the office rooms. "Take a seat, Jimmy," he said. "We need to talk about your stay. You'll be here for six weeks."

"Like fuck I am," I thought, "as soon as I get my break I'm off. This place is nasty."

The man carried on, talking about what the place had to offer me. I just nodded then the talk was over.

The other staff member turned and left me there.

So, I was in a new place. My life was to start again.

*

We walked through a doorway into another section of the building. The man said that was where the older boys stayed. We continued down the long hallway to another part, where I would apparently be with my own age group.

There were about nine boys in my group. We all ate together in a little dining room and we stayed in one huge bedroom. You had a bed and a wardrobe and there were massive windows with bars across them, which, unfortunately, didn't open wide enough for anyone to climb out.

There was a fire door at the end of the hallway and an office. We also had a TV room. It was quite basic, really.

A black Labrador knew Saint Vincent's as its home. The dog stank.

There was a big sports hall for the kids to use, just not my unit. A boot room led out into a little park with swings. It was a big, old place. Creepy.

Almost instantly the bullying and abuse began. The staff would hit us on the head with their knuckles. One member of staff went further (I'd love to name him); he'd kick and punch the boys and make them do things they didn't want to do. If you resisted, he'd set on you and encourage the other lads to fight you, too. You'd be dragged into the sports hall where the other kids would be waiting to jump you. The staff would just stand there and watch you get beaten up by at least eight other boys.

The place was hell.

Staff would follow you into the shower and slap your privates. They thought it was funny.

The abuse was shocking. The staff had free rein to run Saint Vincent's how they wanted.

People on the outside assumed you were a bad kid when they found out you came from there. The place had a reputation.

Whilst there, in the daytime, I attended a school called Clarence House in Freshfield. The other pupils hated the boys from Saint Vincent's. They'd take our pumps and make us walk around the large yard in our bare feet.

I was beaten up so badly I was sick. Then I was made to stand in a corner all day long.

At times I'd see male members of staff with their arms around young girls; sometimes, they'd kiss them. I thought this was normal—I didn't know any better at the time.

The girls lived at Clarence House, which housed boys, too. There was a lot of that there, staff holding hands with the girls, but as I wasn't there all the time, I don't really know what happened to anyone.

In Saint Vincent's I made some friends. We'd run off together. We'd sometimes do wrong together.

I can only speak for myself, but I never experienced any sexual abuse in there, just systematic beatings and bullying, which is just another type of abuse. I knew it was wrong, but I just had to get on with it, or I'd be called a snitch and it would lead to a lot worse.

I was always running away from Saint Vincent's. At one point, my aunt, my dad's sister, tried to get me out of there. She saw what it was like…the older kids and the staff bullying the younger ones.

The staff were just allowed to walk away. They even took money from the kids that were a bit better off. Other staff would give kids cigarettes to batter their housemates. They'd hit them for nothing and attack them in their beds as they slept.

I'd seen it all. There was no chance I was staying there. I'd run away every week, away from the rundown mess of a home and the bullies in charge of it.

Me and a few other boys planned our escape. We prepared to smash the place up and run away during the mayhem. And that's what we did; we smashed every window in the unit and 'ran off on our toes', as we called it.

We planned to get to Liverpool, Manchester, Wales or Birkenhead—the places we were from. I knew where I was going but we had a rule amongst us: we were all to stick together.

First stop was Manchester, a place called Rochdale, where one of the kids lived. He was older than us. We went to his mum's, who fed us and let us get changed. We hung around, robbed sweets from local shops and were chased by the police.

That's what we did on the run. Only I got caught and was taken straight back to my unit at Saint Vincent's. I was gutted the others had got away whilst I was back in Hell. I was told off, like always. They asked where the others had got to.

"I don't know," I told them. They punched me and kicked me but I still told them nothing. I said I'd been on my own, walking along the streets.

No more was said about it. After a few more slaps across the face and knuckles to the head I was sent to bed, ready for the next set of evil dickheads.

The next day came the same shit. I was taken to the office and poked in the face. "Why did you run off? Don't do it again!"

"Yeah, yeah," I thought. "I've heard it all before. Soon as I get out of this office, I'm off again…"

The place was run by bullies. One time, I was on the phone to my mum, telling her that this Irish member of staff had punched me in the face. The guy heard and snatched the phone off me. "He's lying," the Paddy told my mother. That's all they ever said: "He's a liar!"

*

I can't include every example of abuse I know about in this book, for copyright reasons. Every day the staff in Saint Vincent's thrashed the kids. One member of staff was prosecuted for abusing some boys. He was sentenced to ten years, but what about his other crimes and the other kids he abused? This evil man hurt so many kids, and most instances remain unknown to the police.

One day, he told us to go into the TV room. There were about six of us sat there waiting. He walked in and said, "The five of you that ran off, only four of you came back. The fifth has been found dead in Everton Valley in Liverpool, face down behind a hedge."

Despite this news, I still vowed to escape. Before long I was once again walking along the Leeds-Liverpool canal without a care in the world.

Each time I ran off was freedom from the abusers, but it would soon come to an end when I was caught and taken back. Those dark days will never leave me.

*

Time went on. The abuse continued. I had to just take it on the chin, until one day I was told I was moving.

I was sent to a new place, Red Bank Assessment Centre. I was to stay there for six weeks whilst they evaluated me.

I was happy just to get away from Saint Vincent's.

Chapter Five

As I got older, I continued to be sent from pillar to post, from one care home to another.

I was sorry to leave my friends in the hellhole that was Saint Vincent's, but the day I left for Red Bank was a good one.

I had no family to help me as I packed my bags. This was my third placement, and I tried to ignore the stories about where I was headed.

I looked out of the window as we drove there, wondering if the next place was going to full of abuse and bullying, too. We eventually turned down a busy road on my right then the driver said we'd almost arrived.

I couldn't see much, just a long lane off the main road. I spotted a skinny little man standing in front of a building; he looked to be waiting for me.

There was so much going through my head at this point. We finally pulled up and the skinny guy opened my door. "Get out," he ordered.

The driver held my arm to stop me running off.

I started to cry. "Don't cry, Jimmy," said the skinny guy. "You'll like it here. There are lots of boys just like you. Welcome to Red Bank, your new home."

"Is that right?" I thought. "I'll be right out that door, soon as he goes."

We walked to the door where he shouted goodbye to the driver. I followed him into an office and he gestured for me to sit down. "No," I said. "I've been sat for too long already."

"Sit down!" he screamed.

Next thing I knew was the punch someone threw to the side of my head, which knocked me off my feet.

I picked myself up. I was crying and blood ran down my face. My eye throbbed.

"Now listen to me, boy. You will sit and do as you're told in here." I was dragged to the chair and shoved into it.

As he continued to shout, I never once looked at him or the other members of staff. Eventually, he put his hands round my head and forced me to face him.

I called him all the names under the sun as he screamed in my face. "Now you'll be in the Vulcan unit with boys your own age. If you don't do as you're told, you'll be here in front of me. Do you understand?"

"Yes, sir." That's what we had to call them, sir.

I had no contact with family members; this was nasty.

"Stand up, boy, and follow this member of staff to your unit." This was Hell. I could tell I wasn't going to like Red Bank.

We walked down a long, cold corridor that felt like it went on for miles.

We eventually reached the Vulcan unit. There was a room to the right and a much bigger room to the left. I could also see a shower room from where we stood.

I could feel the evil of the place in my bones.

Two staff members ran the unit. They were typical abusers who knew they would get away with their actions.

I was told again that I'd be there for six weeks. I realise now that they just told me that so I wouldn't run off.

Red Bank was the biggest place I'd stayed in. There were five boys in my unit, the same age as me. There were three units altogether housing children our age. The older kids were in the next unit and some kids older again were in the one next to that.

Halfway up the long, long corridor were a few rubber rooms.

I started to settle in. The other kids in my room asked me where I was from and why I was there, same things they ask everyone when they're new to a place.

For the first few weeks I wasn't allowed out of the unit other than to attend school. Life was shit and I felt like a prisoner.

One female member of staff seemed really nice; they always are until they get to know you, then the abuse starts. I got into my first fight with this male member of staff; he was a big fucker who tried telling me to clean the bogs with a toothbrush.

"Fuck off and do it yourself," was my response.

He got me by my neck and pulled me to the floor then sat on top of me. He began punching me in my side. "Once you get up, you'll do as you're told."

Another warden joined in. "We're going to take you to the shower room. You will clean the bogs with this toothbrush."

"Yeah? We'll see," I shouted.

They dragged me, face down, to the shower room and I was made to clean. They held my hand with the toothbrush in it, forcing me to move it back and forth.

"Fuck off!" I screeched.

Seconds later I was dragged to one of the rubber rooms. They ripped all my clothes off me and stood on them, then they laid into me, punching and kicking.

They left me in that room for days. No food, no clothes. I was still only ten years old. Every time one of the bastards came, they'd drag me round the four walls by my hair. They'd smack my head on the floor and make me stand up all day in the corner; if I sat down, they'd kick and slap me. I didn't sit down for a full day.

This was a regular occurrence during the next three years. Staff member Brooks was female; she was okay when she was on her own, but when she was with one called Zebedee she was nasty. Brooks and I got close once I was out of the rubber room. I had to do as I was told every day and I really tried to contain myself.

Eventually, the time came when I was allowed to go out of the unit to the local swimming hall. I'd see other lads from Red Bank use the opportunity to make a run for it in their shorts and vest.

I planned to do the same one day. "That's how I'm going, right over that field, onto the train tracks and I'm gone, no looking back," I thought.

We came swimming twice a week, so I took my time and waited for the right moment. I didn't even know where I was, but I didn't care. That was one thing I never did…care. I just had to rise out of the dark holes.

Most days in Red Bank were the same. The nights were the worst. Some nights I didn't sleep, I was so scared.

The night staff would sneak up to my bed and pull me out. They'd put their hand over my mouth and motion for me to be quiet. They'd smell of beer and cigarette smoke.

They'd take me to the rubber room and beat me for hours. "You're a little bastard," they'd say. This went on for weeks. Sometimes I could hear other kids screaming, so I knew it wasn't just me that they were beating up.

One night I was made to watch them kick ten bells out of one lad. He passed out, there was blood everywhere. They did the same to me and made other lads watch. As they kicked the fuck out of me, they warned the others to say nothing, otherwise they'd suffer the same treatment. I don't know who the lads were, I could just hear them crying.

Chapter Six

I stood three long years of that shit then things changed. I was sent to Liverpool, to an IT centre. That got me out, at least, and was time away from the beatings, but it never lasted long.

The first day away from the unit, when I came back, they were waiting for me. Two fucking abusers with that look on their faces; you knew what was going to happen. Once inside, they ripped my clothes from me and made me stand in my underwear for hours without food. Afterwards, the beating I got was out of this world, and for no reason. Some days I was beaten so badly I couldn't walk. My legs would be black and blue from where they'd kicked me.

Days went by. I'd be locked in a rubber room and starved. Made to stand for hours on end on cold floors.

"Shut up, don't tell anyone." There were their words to me as they walked away.

It became an everyday thing. I was lost in the care system. No one cared—why would they? No one even knew what we were going through.

Some days were better than others. I did woodwork and metalwork, and I enjoyed swimming. I even practiced a bit of reading and spelling.

I hated the school but had to go, regardless. I was marched there…no way out of it, down the long hallway that went on for miles; there were classrooms at the end of it.

You'd be told to get on with your work. If you were good, the teacher gave you a cigarette. He'd sit us down and say, "Don't end up in prison." We all liked Mr Roberts. He was an old man, but he had loads of respect for us, and he never bullied anyone. He'd tell us stories about the other kids that had been at Red Bank and who had now left.

Though I liked Mr Roberts I could not bring myself to tell him what was going on in the home, i.e. the beatings. Even though most of the boys hated schooling, we all went to get away from the unit staff.

As time went on, I tried to do all I could to stop getting a beating. My mother even came for some daft meeting about home leave. I wasn't arsed about home leave by that time, I'd had too many years of being let down.

After so many years of care home abuse I was one hard faced boy. The staff knew it. I could take the abuse and I'd tell them what I thought. However, not once did I ever experience any sexual abuse. I think they saw me as too loud, too clever; they only sexually abused the vulnerable—the boys who were too scared to even talk about themselves, let alone any wrongdoing.

They were the boys who never joined in any sports. They just sat back…the loners. The staff knew which boys to pick on.

More months went by, and after a few meetings with my mother and staff members, I was told I could move to the training unit, where you could do things like cooking, going out, shopping, or more sports. You were also allowed to smoke in there.

"That sounds like fun," I thought, so I kept my head down. "In a few weeks I could be there, doing what all the others do." I'd heard good things about the training unit, and I felt my days in Vulcan were numbered. The beatings had reduced and getting into the training unit was my goal.

I'd not had news or visits from any of my family, but given that it had been six years, I put down to 'shit happens'. My days spent in care had been the worst time of my life as a young boy. Sometimes I didn't even care what day it was, I just had to get on with it and hope I wouldn't be dragged away for a beating.

The day came to move into the training unit. "Bye bye, abusers," I thought to myself as I packed up my little bag of things. I followed Brooks, the female who had abused me in the past with her kicks and hateful slaps; though I was angry I just continued to walk behind her. The training unit was on the same grounds as Vulcan, so it wasn't much of a walk.

She turned to me. "Remember what happened in the rubber rooms? It can soon happen again if you step out of line. Do you understand me?"

"Yes, miss," I said, "I'll be good, miss."

"You better had be. I don't want to see you over in my unit again." Her face softened. "I'll come and visit you when I can."

*

There were lots of older boys in the training unit. Plenty to do and more freedom.

I was shown my room. It was okay, more like a home than a unit placement. I suffered no abuse there, though I did get into a few fights with other boys, and I did run away a few times with some of the others.

The first time I ran away from that unit I tried the drug acid. It gave me such a good feeling that I did it again. On acid I saw things like Mars bars walking down the road, and chickens without heads running after me.

Once I got in with the older lads, I started smoking pot. I never really liked it, so I didn't continue.

After a few months in the training unit I was asked by the staff if I wanted to leave. They mentioned a new place called Bryn Melyn, near Bala, North Wales. It sounded good, so I said okay.

I was about fourteen by this time. The day came and when I thought I was leaving everything about Red Bank behind I found out that Brooks was coming, too. I could not forget what she did to me. Was she following me to make sure I didn't say anything?

At least I wasn't in her unit, where she would be free to beat me with other members of staff.

My new placement was lovely, so much like a real home. I had my own bedroom that looked over massive fields at the back. We called staff by their first names.

In my first week I was in a room with some of the other Bryn Melyn kids and the staff asked if I thought I'd like it there. "Yes, I like it," I said. I was to have a three-day trial run and if everything went well, I'd be allowed to stay.

The trial passed and I settled in as a permanent inmate. I'd not been there long when, one day, I was walking up the stairs as another boy was coming down them. He stopped and said, gruffly, "Come to my room and I'll show you my posters."

I said, Yeah, alright…" and punched him in the mouth.

I knew I'd done wrong, but I never knew what people really meant. In my eyes he was trying it on with me and I didn't want any of the other boys to see me as a little faggot. "Don't even try any of your crazy shit with me. I'm not new to this care home life, I've been in it for years, so fuck off and leave me alone," I'd say.

I was left alone, free to do what I liked, within reason. I got to drive a tractor—a Scouse boy from the streets, in Wales for the first time and driving a tractor…now that was something!

I even tried magic mushrooms fresh from the fields. One of the boys at Bryn Melyn became like a best friend in there to me. "Jimmy, come on, let's go find some magic mushrooms," he said one day.

Me being me, I'd try anything once. I was straight out into the fields, caked in cow shit, picking these mushrooms. I ate them as I picked them and lost count of how many I had. Before long I was tripping, big style. The cows had hands and feet and they were dancing in the fields.

"This shit is good!" I had a great time, not a care in the world.

Next thing we knew, we heard voices coming our way. "Hey! What you both doing there? Get in!"

"Shit." A member of staff had seen us picking mushrooms.

We were still off our heads as we were marched up the hill. We couldn't deny it, we were covered in cow shit, tripping over imaginary obstacles and seeing things running around. When we got to the house, I looked at one of the wardens and his face looked to be melting.

The staff never really cared what we did, as long as it was kept to a level. That's what I liked, until the meetings started.

We started being pinned down and abused, just like in the other homes. We were made to do things we didn't want to, like clean out the cow and pig huts.

I said no. My game was to chase the pigs and kick the chickens and put the cow shit in the other boys' bedrooms. I wasn't there to clean up cow shit and pig shit and look for chickens' eggs.

My mate in there was older than me. He had a girlfriend that sometimes stayed at the home.

"That's what I need," I thought. "I need to do my own thing and have a nice room."

The other boy got drunk one night, so I tried drinking, too. I met his girlfriend's sister and we took off together. It was nice—him with his girl and me with mine, beers coming in through the window as the girls walked in through the front door.

Unfortunately, drink seemed to cause problems with the lad. He'd always end up kicking off and getting pinned to the floor and the girls would be asked to leave by staff.

One night a different boy came to my room. "Follow me," he said. "Watch. I'll make us money."

I jumped out of bed and followed him as he snuck round corners. He crept into the main man's kitchen and we saw his fat wallet just looking at us.

We dropped to our hands and knees to take the wallet off the side. The boy shoved it down his pants. We crept back to bed like nothing had happened. I was fourteen and the other boy was eighteen.

Next thing, the bedroom door flew open and I was yanked out of bed. The main man was going crazy at me. "Where's my wallet? Where's my wallet?!"

"I don't know, sir, I haven't moved out my bed all night."

"You're lying," he screamed, as he pulled me into the main office.

As I walked in the older lad lay twisted on the floor.

"Tell us what happened."

"I told you, I was in bed. I don't know what you're talking about."

The boy was removed from the place, never to be seen again. I was gutted but they told me I was next if anything like that happened again.

*

Our days started at seven, if we were arsed to get out of bed; otherwise, we were dragged out of them by the staff. We had jobs to do for 'spends'. I didn't need spends, I had ways to get what I needed. I didn't smoke, didn't drink, so why did I need spends? I wasn't cleaning up pig shit for ten quid a week.

All the boys had to attend these 'meetings'. We'd sit in a room with the staff then the boss would come in and start with stress relief programmes. These consisted of a boy being held down and made to cry. That boy was Jimmy, every fucking week. Pinned down by three big men as all the other boys watched; they made me cry and called it 'anger relief'.

To me it was called fucking bullying.

I felt lost. Care home staff could do as they pleased. The place wasn't government run, it was private, so visits from the Home Office were announced. This is how they covered things up. They intimated that it was a lovely placement for young boys.

There were no girls in Bryn Melyn. My first Christmas there was crazy. A new woman had joined the staff team. She liked me more than she should have; even though I had a girlfriend, which she knew about, things got out of hand. She was about twenty-five, a nice woman at first then the fun and games started.

She'd take me to town shopping and hold my hand, like I was her boyfriend. On one day trip she pulled into a layby and pulled out a joint. I was shocked at this, but felt much happier about it after smoking the spliff.

She kissed me. "Don't say anything, James. I'll look after you."

I was in the front seat of her car, kissing her like a girlfriend. I was still only fourteen. So wrong, and she knew it was, but she wasn't bothered one bit. She knew I'd never say anything, and even if I did, she'd just claim I was lying and I'd end up being moved yet again. So, I kept quiet.

One night she'd been out with three other lads from the home. They'd been smoking pot and they all came back high. The other staff members knew it, and I knew it.

"I hope you know you're going to get sacked," I warned her. "The boys will say that you gave them the pot."

The shit hit the fan that night. I don't know what started it, but the boot of her car was smashed open by some of the other boys who were looking for her pot.

The police were called, and all hell seemed to break out. But nothing came of it and it was brushed under the carpet like most things in care homes. A few days passed and she came into a room whilst I was alone.

She closed the door and walked up to me. "I'm sorry," she said, "you did tell me and I didn't take any notice." She kissed me on the lips then put her hand down my pants, saying sorry again. A boy saw her kissing me through the window; he told the others and she was asked to leave or face the sack.

She left so that her record remained clear. I heard the manager telling her it was 'off the books'.

The owner of Bryn Melyn was never there, which meant the staff did their own thing. There was one called Adrian who was a pisshead. He took us out in the car, most of the time still pissed.

The first time I got in his car we went to pick up one of the boy's girlfriends. Adrian crashed, pissed up. We all had to say a sheep ran into the road and he'd had to swerve to miss it. Bullshit, he was off his face.

He told us not to say a word to any other staff member. I remember it like it was yesterday. In the end he was sacked for his drinking problem. Only the kids that were in the car with him that night knew about the crash.

I'd been left with a banging head and a lump where I'd hit the window.

*

A new boy came to the home. He knew how to pinch cars and this is where my car crimes first started. We'd take to the streets after midnight; one time we came across a Montego Efi, which was a fast car back in the day. He popped the lock, got in the driver's seat and I climbed into the passenger side. The car started, the lights came on and we were off.

The funny thing was, we could only just see over the steering wheel. This boy knew his shit when it came to stealing cars. I hadn't done anything like that before, but I soon caught up and became a driver overnight.

We headed to Bala without a care in the world and made a few stops at different girls' houses, showing off really. We soon got fed up, though; we hid the car just up the road from the kids' home and went to bed like nothing had happened.

That night I woke to loud banging on my door. It was the police.

"Fuck off! I'm asleep. I've been here all night. I'm not opening my door, so piss off."

"James…just open it, otherwise we'll kick it in."

"Kick it in then, like I really care."

Bang! The door flew open and I jumped up. A copper—PC Jones, being Welsh—screamed, "Get dressed, you little cunt. You've stolen a man's car from up the road and hid it in the lane." He slapped me, the fucking knobhead.

He took me and the other boy to the car. "You were seen in it. And he was driving." He pointed to the other boy.

"I don't think so, PC Jones," I said. "I've not been out my bed all night. Whoever said I was in that car is lying." I walked off, giving the copper a cheeky smile. "What you going to do about it?" I thought to myself.

He made me walk back to the kids' home. By then, members of staff were stood around, just waiting to tell me off. I was getting older now and just wanted to do my own thing. I never listened to them. I hated them all for the simple reason they were all the fucking same…they always had to say something to piss me off, just so they could pin me down and bully me like the arseholes they were.

*

I liked Bala but the locals hated us lads from Bryn Melyn. It had a bad name before I even got there.

I don't know what the other boys were there for, but there was this one lad who was really strange. He was older and looked like a 'wrong 'un'. "Why you here?" I'd say to him.

He'd just walk away, saying "I'll tell on you," like most little faggots did in them places. This one day me and a lad from Manchester popped the window to this strange boy's flat. We let ourselves in; we just wanted to see what his flat was like. As we sneaked around the corner to the stairs, I could hear that someone was there. I popped my head round the corner and saw the older boy standing there with his penis out and a younger boy messing with it.

That was the first time I'd ever come across that shit. I punched the older boy in the face, and we dragged him down the stairs. He got a right beating from us and some of the others—one boy jumped off the stairs onto his head and another kicked him in the face, leaving an imprint of his shoe in the lad's skin.

In our eyes, that type of thing was just not on. No one believed us when we told the staff what we'd seen. After that I started going off the rails. I'd just walk out and stay in Bala, drinking and getting into shit. I knew things like that went on, boys on boys. If you were caught, you could expect a beating off all the lads—we stuck together, no matter what.

The older boy was left for dead that day, he was beaten so badly. He was immediately shipped out for his own safety; we never saw him again.

Me and the boy from Manchester were like brothers. We even had the same haircut, the same clothes. We'd give the same cheek to members of staff. His car robbing got the better of him, though. He loved it and kept doing it, and eventually he was removed to somewhere else. Another friend gone. That's what happened: one day you were there, the next you weren't. There was a lot of shipping around, particularly the boys who were sexually abused. Out of sight, out of mind—both the boy and the staff member concerned.

You knew this type of abuse went on in the homes, you could just tell. Staff would put their arms around the boys they were abusing and find any excuse to touch them. I'd have kicked off so loudly if any of them had tried to touch me.

The owner of Bryn Melyn lived on site with his wife and three kids. I didn't speak to them much. Those kids weren't like us, they had everything. "Spoilt brats," I used to shout, "you're living off my beatings."

When I lost the plot, everyone knew about it. I wrecked the place one night, smashed it to bits. Every window, every door got smashed. I was like a madman—if it could be smashed, it got smashed. I just flipped.

I'd had it with care homes and the fucking bullying. I'd not seen my mother in years when they brought her in to see me. I didn't even like her, she'd put me in care to be kicked and punched. "Why's she here," I thought. "It's been eight years now, and not once has she come before." Even when she rang, she'd say, "No, you can't come home." To this day I don't know why. We still don't speak.

I was soon to be sixteen, an age where I'd be able to walk out of care and live with my girlfriend. As it got closer to my birthday, I picked up a few charges from the police for damage and assaults—these wouldn't be the only things on my record as life went on.

In preparation, I moved into the 'flat'. It was still part of the home, but I was able to do my own shopping and stuff. They were gearing me up for the big wide world. I even got a job—chainsaw felling—with a staff member. I did it for a few weeks, but they didn't give me any more money.

I hated farming shit. "It's not my game," I'd tell them. I did learn a few things during my time in care; I could read and write, for example, considering I never went to a mainstream school. If they ever tried to send me to one, I'd kick off and give the staff so much abuse it was unreal. I took all my anger out on them, but that's what they got paid for, in my mind.

I kept saying, "When I'm sixteen, watch me walk right out of here and give you the middle finger. There'll be fuck all you can do."

I was going out with a girl from Bala and the care home's manager said I could go live with her when I was of age. We'd been together for three years; she was my mate's girlfriend's sister.

We stayed together right up to the day I left the home.

There was a holiday planned for the boys around the time of my sixteenth birthday. The owner said to me, "Do you want to go on this holiday or leave care?"

"Stick your holiday up your arse. Come the 16th, I'm out of here." What did he think I'd say? "Yeah, give me the holiday of a lifetime. Yes, please." Fuck off, no holiday in the world would beat the day I'd walk free of the abuse.

He took nine lads away on holiday and I was left there on my own. It was four days until my birthday and the day I would finally be out of that place. No staff, no abuse. Freedom was getting closer, I could smell it.

All the paperwork was written up and there it was: I was signed out of care and free to live with my girlfriend. I received no help, no funds, fuck all—they just left me to it.

I had no back up plan, either. I was out in the big, bad world, with no one but my girlfriend and her dad. If our relationship broke down, I had no one and nothing.

Did anyone in the care home care that I had gone? I think they were glad I'd left. There was nothing they could do to me now and they knew it.

I knew about my rights in care and I was too clever for them, so they couldn't touch me. It was best that they let me go.

So, I went to live with my girlfriend and her family. No contact from anyone…staff members, homes, Sefton social workers; they never cared anyway. I had that many of them I lost track. They were full of shit, every one of them. They did a shit job; not once did I see one after I left, and I had no funding from them. A waste of the air we breathe, those bastards did nothing to help me.

I got a job with my girlfriend's dad in a steelwork factory, drilling steel pins. I had to make a go of it; Bryn Melyn lads had a bad name with locals. I had to show them I was different, not the little shithead who would rob your cars, smash your town up and give you abuse. This is what I had to deal with, at first, from many of the locals, but my girlfriend's dad was well respected.

"Leave Jimmy alone," he'd say to them. "He's a good lad. He's with my daughter and he works."

I kept my head down and did as I was told for a good few months, staying out of shit. No police, nothing.

One summer's night I got drunk with a local boy, down at the lake. Me and him swam out to the rowing boats visitors paid to use. I made it to the first boat. It was chained up to about nine others.

I sank it. It pulled another boat down with it…one boat, two boats… "Shit, what have I done?" I swam back to the bank and watched all the boats sink.

It was funny at the time, but then the police came and we got done. It was my first court case. I'd been in trouble before, but I'd never been charged.

When I was six, I remember my mum taking me to the police. "Can you put him in your cells and show him what it's like?" she asked the coppers.

"Go on then, take me. I'm not arsed," I said. I did not give two fucks about the police as a boy.

I stood in a courtroom in Bala, charged with conveyance taken without authority under the Theft Act 1968 s.12 9 (1) 20/06/91.

The outcome was a twelve-month conditional discharge.

On 20/08/91 I was charged with theft from a vehicle; I received twelve months' disqualification from driving and my licence was endorsed twice—even though I didn't even have a licence.

In Bala court on the 20/11/91 I was given another twelve-month conditional discharge and a month concurrent, for handling stolen goods. My record was building up fast, not that I cared.

On my ninth court case, on 21/11,91, for again taking conveyance without authority, the fucker residing sent me to a young offenders' institution for twenty-eight days. A second charge of criminal damage and assault occasioning actual bodily harm brought another twenty-eight days.

Fifty-six days. My first time 'away', I was placed with over two hundred lads in HM Prison Werrington, a male-only juvenile prison in Staffordshire.

The institution stated: 'To give young people the best chance to turn their lives around by providing them with safe, decent and secure environments that focus on education and personal development and empower them to make positive change, to successfully return to the community and lead law-abiding lives.'

But not Jimmy. I did my time here; all bed packs and marching around, being told what to do. I was then asked if I wanted to go to an open prison.

I said yes. 'The Regime at Thorn Cross provides for a wide range of training and education courses. The emphasis of these courses is to link to either employment or training opportunities on release, while also addressing individual 'Skills for Life' needs. Courses offered include construction crafts, motor vehicles, horticultural courses, hospitality and catering, and rail construction NVQ Level 2.'

Thorn Cross had a number of partnerships with national and local employers that offered opportunities for work placements—prior to, and on, release.

"Sounds good, yes?" they said.

NO! I ran off soon as I got there. I saw the open doors and legged it. "See yer," I shouted, giving them the finger.

I hitched lifts from Thorn Cross to Chester, then to Wrexham and back to Bala. It wasn't the first time I'd done that.

I made it to my girlfriend's house, but I knew the police would be looking for me. I lasted about a week on the run before I was caught and taken back to Thorn Cross.

I was locked up on the block and fourteen more days were added to the time I had to serve.

This time I stayed. It was okay once I got used to it. They had all sorts there: sports, hovercrafts, shops, and gardening…even though I hated it. Plus, I had my own room with a key, so I could come and go and lock my door.

Whatever the place said it did, all I seemed to experience was getting twatted over the head every day with a bunch of keys before being locked in.

I headed to Bala on my release and settled back into life with my girlfriend.

It wasn't long, however, before I got into more trouble with the law. On 18/06/92 I was back up in court for handling and theft. I was sent back to Warrington House Young Offenders for fourteen days.

More bed packs, boot room rules and being slapped about.

Home to Bala, then I was charged with assault occasioning actual bodily harm offences. Straight back to Warrington House for eighty-four days. It was the longest sentence I'd had.

The place was nasty, like a boot camp. Around two hundred lads in there for crimes like mine, all counting the days to get home.

We ate together and slept in dormitories that housed twenty to thirty lads at a time. All the beds were in a line down each wall. At night, some of the lads would tip your bed upside down and you'd be trapped. It was funny if it wasn't your bed that got tipped up.

Every lad had to do the 'up and over run'; you'd stand at the end of the line of beds and run over and under them, taking a beating as you did it. You had to do this on both sides of the dormitory. There was always a bigger lad running the dorms, so you just did what he said, otherwise you'd be beaten up by loads of lads. It was just easier to get on with it. Life was hard enough in there as it was without fighting with all the lads. Keeping your head down was the best way to get through your sentence with all your bones intact.

I left there for the second time and tried to get on with my life. This time, when I went back to Bala and my girlfriend, we split up. Our lives had gone in different directions. Mine wasn't heading anywhere good; from what I know, hers was much better—she's now married with children, a nice house and a good job.

It's a shame I never took that path, but by this time, after the care homes, the abuse, the beatings—and now, young offenders to add to my list—I didn't give a fuck about my life.

On 30/09/93 I entered North Sefton District Magistrates' Court charged with burglary and theft. I was sent to Lancaster Farms. I was the sixty-third lad in there; it was a new juvenile jail.

I experienced my first Christmas away in Lancaster Farms. I had four 'failing to surrender to bail' charges and a police assault (which I wasn't guilty of) that were to run concurrently. Every time the police recognised me on the outside they'd pick me up for something daft. Understandably, I'd kick off. I got locked up for assault for three months; an easy conviction and they knew it, the pricks.

I did my time and met up with some old school lads I knew from homes I'd been in. What they'd done was their problem, not mine. The drugs they took was also their problem, not mine. People claimed I was on Class A drugs, but I wasn't—just more bullying tactics.

Admittedly, as time went on and my life continued to spiral, I found the drug ecstasy. I loved it, I was on it every day and night. I smoked pot, too, so most of the time I was high. I tried to make a life for myself and stayed away from the hard stuff; the lads I hung about with went downhill fast to Class A drugs, which was enough to put me off.

I got a flat and moved in. Then I met a scouse girl from Anfield; she was really nice and I fell in love with her. I slowly walked away from the lads I was hanging about with. I had a girlfriend now, that was all I wanted—to settle down and be happy. Even my mum met her.

My girlfriend was stunning: blonde hair, blue eyes, lovely nature. She had a job and nice friends. We went everywhere together; we were very happy. We were together for three years, which were the best three years of my life, after the shit I'd had in the care homes.

I didn't get into any trouble during our relationship. Having the flat made me feel more responsible and after a few weeks she moved in. She was nearer to her mum and everything was looking up for once.

My mother even made an effort, helping me to sort my flat. The lads I'd been hanging around with left me to it and wished me luck.

One summer's day I was walking to my mum's house up the road when I saw some lads I knew. They were waving their arms and one lad shouted, "Move! Get out of the way." I slipped down an alleyway and waited for a few minutes before slowly heading towards them.

"A silver XR3i full of fellas was looking for you," one lad said.

"I don't know what that's about."

"It's Tony the Greek," he said.

"I've never met him in my life." I continued walking, next thing I knew there was a loud screech of tyres at the corner of the street. I heard them coming but I didn't see them, as I ran as fast as I could towards my mum's.

A man got out of the car and started chasing me, yelling, "I kill you, I kill you, cunt!"

I went white. I remember thinking, "I can't go the front way, he'll get me." I headed towards the back of the houses and over a big gate. He was lost, he clearly didn't know his way around. I was safe.

I sat for a few seconds, which felt like half an hour. Eventually, I pulled myself up to the top of the gate and jumped down the other side, walking slowly to the end of the path.

I turned right; my mum's house was within arm's reach. I rang the bell with urgency. She opened the door and instantly cottoned on that something was happening.

The crazy man ran up the path behind me, still screaming. He whacked me on the back with a fuck off slab of concrete.

My mum started screaming her head off. I didn't even know what was going on or why. Mum dragged me inside by the arms. The man fucked off.

Then she got on my case, saying, "What was that about? You must know."

"I don't. I don't even know them. I've not done anything, they're just after me. I've been with my girlfriend for days, I've not seen anyone. Whatever it is, someone's lied about it and put my name in the hat for it."

My mum got straight on the phone to the police. I kept saying I didn't know anything. I knew to keep my head down until I found out more.

All through the summer these guys chased me round in their silver XR3i, shouting abuse at me. Still no one knew why. They were Turks; I was only 19, they were grown men.

It was only a matter of time until they got to me. People told them to leave me alone but they'd just get abuse back, too. My mum flapped about, saying, "Stay in, don't go anywhere," but I had my own place and I wanted to go home.

I decided to chance it. I met with my mate, Kevin, and talked away about my new place. I invited him and another friend, Mary, to see it. We all walked to the block of flats, got the lift to the thirteenth floor then headed to my front door.

Inside, I put the kettle on, still chatting away. "Oh, I've no milk."

"I'll run to the shop," said Kevin.

"Okay, mate, nice one." I looked out of the window, enjoying the view on such a clear day. You could see over to Liverpool and Seaforth docks, being so high up.

Mary put some music on and a few minutes passed. Then she heard Kevin shouting me. "JAY, JAY!"

We turned the tunes off and looked out the window. Kevin was on the ground, shouting, "Get out the flat! Get out the fucking flat now, they're all on their way up! The Greeks!"

"Fucking hell!" We ran to the door. As I opened it this cunt punched me in the face. He dragged me to the front room then started kicking me.

Four of them beat me up. There was blood everywhere, up the freshly painted walls, all over the new carpets. I passed out and still they carried on.

My face was black and blue. I was out cold; I didn't know what was going on around me. Eventually, the men got back in the lift, leaving Mary and I alone. She couldn't escape in the lift—they jammed the door with a Coke can, which gave them more time to get away.

Mary saw everything, the poor thing. She took the stairs all the way to the ground floor and ran to the man in the office. "Please, please, ring the police! My mate's been badly beaten up in his flat."

The police came and I was taken to hospital. Apparently, I was lucky to be alive.

Four grown men jumping on my head and punching me in the face…shocking. My first proper beating, but I was used to it—after all, I'd had that many in the care homes.

"Fuck it," I thought. "Fuck them as well."

My mum came to the hospital, but I was in such a bad way I couldn't comprehend what was going on around me. My lip was sewn up. All my front teeth had been knocked out and the bones in my mouth shattered. For what reason?

Once I was well enough I left hospital to stay at my mum's. Police came to interview me. They were everywhere, with guns and bulletproof jackets on. Things were fucking heavy, and I still didn't know what it was all about. No one did, only the ones who did it.

"Who was it?" the police asked me. "Who the fuck did this to you, lad?"

They knew who it was, everyone did, but I didn't tell them fuck all.

"Tell them now," said my mum. "If you don't, you can get out and I'll wash my hands of you." I had no choice but to leave.

Police cordoned off the streets around my mum's house as I left.

A few days went by and I healed fast. The police were going after the Greeks for attempted murder. A big jail sentence was coming their way. They'd been caught on CCTV coming into the building and leaving.

I didn't give a statement for weeks and weeks, but the Greek cunt kept coming at me. In the end he got picked up and kept in the cells. He was charged and bailed but the charges were dropped. I had to. He'd paid other people to kidnap me.

I was walking along the road with my girlfriend and she stopped to talk to a girl she knew. I kept walking. I looked back; she was still talking so I carried on. As I walked under a bridge two cars pulled up. One was the white XR3i.

"Don't run, lad," one of them shouted, so I just stood there. "Come with us, nothing will happen." Someone grabbed my arm and pushed me into the white escort. Luckily, my girlfriend had seen what had happened. She panicked and called the police. They scoured everywhere, looking for me in this white car.

I hid my gold ring and my bracelet in case they decided to take them, but they'd not snatched me to rob me. They were taking me to speak to the main guy who left me for dead…to intimidate me so I'd drop all the charges.

They drove around, looking for a house to put me in, but the lad who lived in the house they took me to said he didn't want to get involved.

They took me to a phone box and rang the Greek fella. I had to speak to him. "Drop all the charges," he said, "the men who have you aren't fucking around."

"Okay, okay," I said. They then drove me to Waterloo Police station.

"Get out and go in," they ordered.

I did as I was told and dropped the charges. Case closed.

Many years later, I spoke to the Greek guy again. He was so sorry. "Jay, I mean this from the bottom of my heart, may I drop down dead," he said. "We were told a pack of lies."

Despite what some people may believe, I never took a penny off him for what he did to me. Anyone who thinks I robbed him and did something bad, that's the fucking truth.

I moved to Anfield with my girlfriend, but things were difficult. I didn't want to go anywhere or do anything. I did try to change but it never worked. Eventually, we split up and I had to move into my dad's place. It was a fucking nightmare. I got into shit with people…suffered lies, threats, bullying. In the end I flipped and went mad. I pulled all the bin bags out into the road, blocking all routes round Seaforth. It was bin collection day and I went on a one-man riot.

I headed to the big social workers' offices in Crosby and told them I needed their help after all the abuse and shit I'd been left to deal with. I felt that they owed me.

I smashed the fire alarms on all the floors and all two hundred employees were forced to come outside. "You're all fucking wrong 'uns, every fucking one of you. One day I'll prove it."

This was during rush hour. The busy South Road was blocked with cars, the police, firemen…it was madness. I stood on a wall and shouted, "You fucking pricks!" Nine years of anger I had for them twats came flooding out. They knew why I was there. I wanted my care home files. I wanted the facts.

The police said I was crazy. I told them all about the abuse I'd suffered. They took me to hospital, claiming I was ill.

They just wanted me locked up, shut away, so my story would never come out. Abuse was not just confined to the homes; the fucking police abused their power as well. I've received a good few kicks and punches from the Crosby police, the dirty bastards.

We made our way to a place called Stoddard House, where I got a Section 2 assessment to see if I was fucking loony. I was kept there for two weeks until they kicked me out and said there was nothing wrong with me. "He's just angry because of Sefton's social workers and the abuse he went through in care homes," they said.

I must admit, I was looked after in there. Fresh fruit and prawn salad every day, and the student nurses were gorgeous. They looked after me as well, didn't give me any medication. I'd seen others walking about like they had no soul.

I went back to Seaforth and got a nice flat in Bower Grove—same road as my dad, that's the only reason I got it, really. Then fucking shit started with the local fucking bullies who had nothing better to do. Groups of five or ten lads would jump me and tell lies to other people about me. I find it so fucking funny to this day that they never got fuck all out of me.

Eventually I had to move out; I never felt safe there. I went to Liverpool where I met an amazing woman called Betty Thomas in the White Chapel Centre. She's not there now—that place will never be the same again.

She knew I was a good kid and she helped me get past what I was going through. Mental health workers were trying to get me to see all kinds of people, so I could be carted off. I was on thin ice…trust me, I knew too much and was about to blow everything out of the water. Every care home in Liverpool was going to get it.

I had no time for trouble—I had bigger and better things to do. I planned to write this book all those years ago. People would say, "Get it done, Jimmy lad, it needs to be out there. Fuck all the haters."

There was one woman who knew me as a child. She was called Patsy. She was hard as fuck, you didn't upset her. She was like the queen bee of Seaforth.

I loved her. She said it how it was. There were a few others I loved, but there was far more of them who were knobheads.

Everyone in Seaforth knew I was sick, but they thought it was down to drugs. I wasn't even on any drugs at the time, I'd just had it with everything.

Chapter Seven

The last straw came when the police got hold of me through the dole office. I received a letter from Operation Care about the abuse. This was the first time anyone in authority had ever sent me anything about it. The shit was about to hit the fan, big time.

The police wanted to come and see me; someone somewhere must have given them my name. I contacted them from my dad's place.

I'd come to hate the police, but I felt I had to see them. If there was a chance I could help others—or even myself—it was worth a try.

I didn't trust them. Can you blame me? I didn't trust many people, really, after what I'd been through. The police came. They sat down with me, chatted a bit then asked me some questions. Little of what they had to say made any sense. I told them things, they asked me about names of staff and homes I'd been in. I wanted to tell them about the abuse, but I was in a mess. I was heading for a breakdown…the police, care homes, the bullying, people thinking I had money—it was really getting me down.

The outcome of the operation will follow: the facts about certain care home, the abusers who got jail. This information comes from the whitepaper report, i.e. facts. It's not my opinion, it's what the government did.

It is, according to a government minister in the House of Lords, 'the greatest scandal of the 20th century'. Unfortunately, the minister's view has not found much echo in society at large. The story has been largely ignored by the press. It has, too, been the subject of little academic research, despite the obvious need for a greater understanding. Successive governments have commissioned reports into particular incidents, but most of these have been at a local level. Yet the importance of understanding the wider history of these scandals cannot be overstated, for without such understanding, it is impossible to frame a policy to tackle the problem.

The report validates my story. There has been a huge cover up. The abusers have been carrying out their crimes for years.

There a list of twenty-eight missing people who are being sought by the Department of Health after the Waterhouse report; it includes some of the most dangerous and notorious paedophiles involved in the scandal. It also includes the names of a handful of people who were exonerated. Among them is David Gwyn Birch, from Bryn Estyn, and Christopher Ian Thomas, from Little Acton.

Malcolm Ian Scrugham, who was jailed for ten years in 1993 for raping a foster child over several years from the time she was eleven, has vanished. So has Kenneth Andrew Scott, of Tanllwyfan, who was jailed for eight years in

1986 for buggery and gross indecency with three boys aged fourteen to sixteen. He was later employed as a warden of a youth hostel.

Gary Cooke was a member of the paedophile ring in the Wrexham area based around the Crest Hotel, a public lavatory and the Lift Project, which helped young homeless people. He was jailed for five years in 1980 for buggery, indecent assault and taking an indecent photograph.

Maurice (Matt) Matthews (Bryn Estyn) used unjustified force against children in three isolated incidents.

Paul Bicker Wilson (Bryn Estyn): suspended two-year jail sentence for physical assaults on boys.

Stephen Norris: (Bryn Estyn): seven years' imprisonment for buggery and indecent assault of six boys.

(Joseph) Nefyn Dodd (Ty'r Felin): frequently used excessive physical force on children. Huw Meurig Jones (Little Acton): not suitable to be employed in residential care or social service work with children.

Carl Johnson Evans (Little Acton): written warning after admitting unauthorised fieldwork visits to an adolescent girl in care. John Ilton (Bryn Estyn): disciplinarian teacher who lacked self-control when physically confronting boys.

Jacqueline Elizabeth Thomas (Chevet Hey): three months' suspended prison sentence for indecently assaulting a fifteen-year-old boy.

David John Gillison (Bersham Hall): three-and-a-quarter years' imprisonment for gross indecency with a sixteen-year-old boy. Heather Patricia Lynn (Cartrefle): sexual intercourse with a sixteen-year-old boy in care.

Joan Glover (South Meadow): character defects meant she 'lost her rag' and slapped children. John Ernest Allen (Bryn Alyn): six years' imprisonment for indecent assaults on six boys.

Peter Steen (Bryn Alyn): used excessive force to restrain boys and girls. Bryan Davies (Ystrad Hall School): given twelve months' probation for indecent assaults on two pupils. Anthony David Taylor (Bryn Alyn): fined twenty pounds for two indecent assaults on boys.

Iain Muir (Bryn Alyn): jailed for six months for unlawful sexual intercourse with a girl. Leslie Wilson (Little Acton): jailed for fifteen months for indecent assault, gross indecency and attempted buggery.

Michael Taylor (Bersham Hall): cautioned for indecently assaulting four children. Alfred Frederick Tom Dyson (Bryn Estyn): jailed for eighteen months for indecency with a boy. Tom Davies (Bryn Estyn): used physical force inappropriately against boys.

*

These are real-life examples of the abuse I've talked about and the outcomes each one led to. There are still hundreds—maybe thousands— more victims out there who are too ashamed to come forward. I know this for a fact; I speak to them all the time. They might not have known where to turn before now, but this is why I'm writing this book.

These are the people who need the abuse exposed, who need it all out in the open. Children who suffer abuse never forget what's done to them; it can cause them a lifetime of problems.

*

I'm not a liar; here are more facts:
Community Care, Thursday 27th April 2000.

Local authorities paid more than £28 million to the Bryn Alyn community of children's homes, whose owner John Allen was jailed in 1995 for child abuse, it was revealed at the North Wales child abuse tribunal last week.

Allen was at one time drawing an income of more than £200,000 from the operation.

It also emerged that an allegation of abuse at Bryn Alyn was investigated by police in 1970, more than two decades before Allen was jailed for six years.

The tribunal heard how Allen had showered gifts on boys at Bryn Alyn and former residents. Allen told the hearing that an attempt had been made to blackmail him. But Allen, who was brought from Leeds Prison to give evidence to the tribunal, claimed that he was innocent of the charges for which he was jailed and that the allegations against him had been made up.

The tribunal, which is due to finish taking evidence before Easter, heard that one boy had received a total of £25,000 from Allen. It is estimated that the money, gifts and trips given to children by Allen totalled more than £100,000.

"You ran Bryn Alyn to exploit children for your own gratification and to be paid substantial funds. The gifts were given so you could exploit children," said Gerard Elias QC, counsel for the tribunal.

Allen denied that the gifts were to keep children quiet or to enable him to exploit them for his own gratification.

At one stage, the Bryn Alyn community was home to more than two hundred children, who were placed there by thirty-eight different social services departments.

*

Look how many there was. It's evil. No wonder there are so many fucked up adults in this world when you consider what they went through as children. They fucked my life up and all I got was to be put on the sick and told to shut up about it.

Well, fuck them. I want everyone to know that we're not all bums on the fucking dole. Some of us cannot work and don't go out of the house for reasons like this. Maybe now you've read my story you understand.

I only speak for the people that went through such an experience. More happened than the government believes; trust me, I know.

The ones that were abused by the evil, sick Allen didn't get asked about him. He's got away with a lot more than you know. Him and Mr Statton are first class wrong 'uns. But there were many more abusers than them two at Saint Vincent's. It makes me sick thinking about it, but I feel I have to, just to get my point across—not just for me, but for loads more of us. So that our suffering, the nights we cried ourselves to sleep, how we couldn't eat, the horrors and evil these men and women inflicted…so that everything is heard.

None of it is our fault. Please don't judge us. Show us some love.

Anyone could end up in care for any reason. I was just lucky not to be sexually abused, but others weren't so lucky, God help them. I wish those people all the luck in the world. Remember: you're not alone, my friends.

I hope this book is a light at the end of tunnel. Don't give up the fight, I tell myself, every single day and night.

Too many have died. Too many lives have been destroyed. Stop government child abuse cover ups. It's time for the truth.

*

The overwhelming evidence, of course, points to the fact that child sexual abuse is deeply damaging. This has been proved beyond doubt by many researchers. Studies on the impact of child abuse demonstrate a wide range of associations with various disorders and psychiatric conditions. The campaigning group, Accuracy About Abuse, has uncovered studies demonstrating correlations between child sexual abuse and depression, suicidal tendencies, asthma, ulcers, drink and drug addiction, admission to hospital for psychiatric treatment, sexual dysfunctions and many other disorders.

This is what the government has said. This abuse is bigger than a mere slap in the face. It's unconsciously stepping into a world of evilness and horror that children simply cannot understand.

*

By the summer of the year 2000, more than a hundred care workers had been prosecuted. However, there may be up to ten times this number of cases in the pipeline, depending on how some of the big cases pan out. According to evidence given at a trial in June, there have been allegations against ninety-one care workers at St George's (in Formby, Cheshire), alone.

And some investigations—such as those in Lancashire, Somerset and Avon—have barely got going.

So many people in authority knew what was going on but they covered it up. They don't want people to know what happened—and which, probably, is still happening—in these institutions. The children in these care homes are now grown men. Damaged grown men. Damaged from the abuse they received.

These pricks have no right to cover anything up. It's okay for them, they weren't the ones being abused—they just stood back and let it happen. God, give me the power to bring my pain to this book and let everyone see how fucking wrong this all is. This is just the tip of the iceberg, too; I could report much more, but I don't want my story to be overtaken by theirs.

At the White Chapel Centre, away from the bullies, I felt hopeful. Betty Thomas was an angel sent to watch over me; she's like a second mother to me. She loved me and saw me pull through some fucking ugly times: breakdowns, drinking upsets; she helped me through them all.

She'd say, "No, Jimmy, you did it all on your own." But she's wrong. She helped me. Even on the end of the phone, she was there for me, and she always will be. If it wasn't for her I don't know where I'd be today—she's what any mother should be like.

Betty helped me fill out the forms for my old flat and she made phone calls for me. She even gave me her own number. "Ring it anytime you need me, I'll be there." That's all I needed, a mother figure who could see I was a good lad with a good heart, and that I'd just gone down the wrong path.

I managed to pull myself together and stayed with Betty at the White Chapel Centre for nine months. We got my sick money sorted, the doctors…everything I needed to try and have a normal life.

I then moved to the Wirral and stayed with my dad's sister. "I've got some money," I thought, "now's my time to shine." My auntie gave me a roof over my head and I felt safe. I didn't go out much, really, I was still a mess deep down—so much anger and hate…nothing I could do about it, I just had to get on with it. I knew I was ill, but I had to try and keep my head together and not lose it.

I met up with a girl I knew from when I was young, from before I went into care, and we started going out together. She knew I'd been in kids' homes and jail, but she felt that people had the ability to change and move on.

We went to her house for a drink and we talked. She asked me to stay the night and things developed from there. We were together five years and had two kids, a girl and a boy. It was my longest relationship, but it still didn't last. In the end, we just grew apart.

The kids were fine about the split. I know they'll read this one day and learn about my early life in all its glory. I just hope they're proud of what I'm trying to achieve, and that they say, "That's my dad's book!" when they see it. That would be the best day of my life, the recognition that I've achieved something despite my sickness and the horrors I've had to deal with.

I've been left with many problems…my health, not having a normal life, people gossiping—so, here are the facts. Read them. There are things I've not gone into fully for legal reasons, to cover myself, though I've got much more in my files—records from the homes I stayed in, even my medical file and my PNC record that shows everything I've been charged with. I felt I had to keep everything for future verification, should this be necessary.

Once our relationship ended, I moved from house to house, and ended up in Lancashire, a place called Nelson. I stayed with a friend; I had nowhere else to go. I settled there but I wanted my own space and got a house over the road from my mate's.

I've never felt so lonely in all my days, but I was a fighter and I could start all over again, get my life sorted and have a nice house. Wherever I lived, I always made it look smart. I never looked like a tramp; even when I was on the streets in Liverpool, I always looked fresh. No one really knew I was homeless. I fixed up the three-bed house and made friends with some local lads who had motorbikes.

"That's what I need," I thought, so I got one. It was cheap because it had been stolen, but I didn't care—I just wanted one. I collected it from Manchester. My first DT125. "I'm fucking flying now!"

I spent money and time on new plastics for it. I had help from a friend who knew loads about bikes. We brought it into the kitchen and sprayed it up. The bike looked amazing. We put it back together and it purred like a kitten.

I wanted to show it off, so I got it out on the road and kicked it through its gears. I got onto a nearby field, ripping it up and caking the bike in mud. When I headed back to the opening, I found the police had me blocked in. "Come here, you!"

"Fuck this, I'm off." I took off through a bush. They ran after me, but I left them standing. "Fuck off, copper!" I flexed the gears. Brappp, brappp…

"We know where you live!" they shouted after me.

I couldn't go back home with the bike, so I headed onto another pathway. That was when the bike cut out. I was about sixty seconds away from my mate's house. "Shit!" The police were looking for me and I was sat on a stolen bike. I jumped off and started running with it. Looking behind me, I saw two fat coppers coming fast. "Fuck this," I thought. "I'm not dropping my bike."

They got closer and one of the cunts jumped on my back. "Fuck! I'm nicked now."

"Whose is the bike?"

"Mine," I said. "I got it from Manchester. Paid a grand for it, why?"

They checked its numbers and rung it in. "It's been stolen."

I was gutted. The first day I took that bad boy out and it was taken off me by two fat coppers. They didn't take me, as I had paperwork from the lad I'd got it off. I was lucky, they didn't charge me, but there was no getting away from the fact I had no bike and I'd have to walk home.

The bike gone, I went back to being my old self in my new house. It wasn't long after that that I got a car. Fuck walking, I must have had about twenty cars back then—out of one, into another, as easy as that. Not like today, where you can't get away with anything unless you're legal.

I was living in Nelson by now. I knew a few of the lads from various kids' homes; one of the main families were Irish, with six brothers. I'd looked after one of the older ones when I was in Red Bank. He knew I was a good lad, which meant I didn't get any trouble at my door.

*

I've always felt that I had to write this book. I've so much anger and frustration that it's hard to keep a lid on it.

Writing this has brought back some painful memories. Deep, dark hallways of pain and sadness. No young boy should ever go through what we did. That's why I'm messed up; I've carried all this for more than thirty years.

Nothing much has ever been done about it. Yes, some abusers received jail sentences. What's ten years to them, compared to a lifetime of pain for the ones they abused?

They're able to walk the streets and live happy lives. Their victims are the ones with a life sentence…ill, unhappy, no hope, on the sick. Do you think that's fair?

The government has closed the abuse case down. What right do they have to make that decision? Fuck them, it will stay open as long as us, the abused, say so. Those in power just sit there, reading reports. Well, read this, you fucking pricks—the fucking facts from a boy who's seen more and knows more than you ever will.

There were plenty more kids abused, but they're too fucking ashamed to come forward. The ones who closed the case are just concerned with covering their backs and those of their fucking friends that abused their power. The facts are there in black and white in the public report. It's shocking to even read it…abusers getting ten years in prison for abusing more than twenty boys. Boys that never even had the chance to speak up. It's a fucking joke, it gets me so mad.

I know my life has not been the best, but I'm so lucky to even be here writing this. I'm doing it for the boys out there who have asked me to make the real facts public. For the ones that have died and the ones that are so fucked up they don't know what day it is. It's all down to the fucking abusers who did some nasty, evil, wicked things to young boys and got away with it for many years—even before I was in care.

I don't know if these words will be blocked, but I'm going to do my best to get them published and in the public domain.

Chapter Eight

"As survivors and associated professionals, we were very much hoping to take up the invitations to engage with your Ministerial Officers to discuss the Child Sex Abuse Inquiry, but we regret to say we have to decline. We, alongside many survivors, have made numerous representations to you regarding our view that the Inquiry as it stands is not fit for purpose. Its Terms of Reference (ToR) are inadequate for delivering the original declared intentions of the inquiry, namely to investigate government and establishment cover ups of paedophiles in their ranks and aiding bringing the perpetrators to justice.

Secondly, both your appointees to Head the Inquiry Panel have had to be forced out by survivors because of obvious conflicts of interest, and you have failed to address similar issues regarding other Panel appointees.

Thirdly, that the cut-off date for the Inquiry investigations was set at 1970 is highly disturbing given that the 1969 Children's Act transferred Home Office run youth establishments, from which thousands of abuse allegations eventually emerged. It highlights the lack of transparency regarding the Home Office's dealings with the Inquiry, not to mention the apparent obfuscations and manipulations in the defence of the appointment of Fiona Woolf. As a result, the Home Office seems to be running the Inquiry to meet others' needs rather than those of survivors and the public.

We therefore have little option but to end engagement with the Inquiry and call on other survivors, whistleblowers, associated professionals and agencies to follow suit until, as Home Secretary, you:

- announce the scrapping of the current panel and its replacement on a transparent basis
- declare a statutory inquiry
- announce that the TOR will focus on: 1) Organised and Institutional Abuse – hearing evidence from survivors of such abuse 2) Extending the cut-off date to 1945 and linking with Inquiries in other parts of the UK 3) Setting up a dedicated police team at the National Crime Agency to take evidence alongside the inquiry to investigate and prosecute offenders 4) Holding those that have failed in their professional duty or covered up allegations or been obstructive to account.

Yours faithfully,
Andy Kershaw and Tony Martin (Survivors of Forde Park)
Bobby Martin, Gang Intervention Advisor & Islington Care Home Survivor
Luke Payne, Child Trafficking Survivor.
Nigel O'Mara, Former Survivors' Helpline Counsellor/ Public Relations

Officer
Caroline Carnot, Author & Founding Executive Care Leavers Association
Peter McKelvie, Whistleblower and former child protection worker
Dr Liz Davies, Reader in Child Protection, London Metropolitan University
Ruth Stark MBE, President International Federation of Social Workers
Ann Davis, Emeritus Professor of Social Work and Mental Health, University of Birmingham
Phil Frampton (Founding Chair, Care Leavers Association 2000-04)
Stephen Morris, Church of England Children's Society Careleaver
Brian Douieb, Former Leaving Care Social Work Manager
Les Huckfield MP for Nuneaton 1967-83. MEP for Merseyside East 1984-89
Dr Kenneth McIntyre, CPsychol, AFBPsS
Dr Paul Redgrave, Director of Public Health, Barnsley 2004-09
Ed Nixon, Chief Executive, Family Care Associates
Anne Southworth, Senior National Education Specialist (Audit Commission) – Retired
Dr Rachel Chapple, Social Anthropologist, Founder, Real Stories Gallery Foundation
Councillor Ann Kerrigan
Ann Mallaby, Justice Campaigner
Andrea Enisuoh, Community Organiser, Hackney Unites
Miriam Day, Writer and survivor of childhood sexual abuse
Robert Chewter, Campaigner

*

Fiona Woolf is following in the footsteps of Elizabeth Butler-Sloss with a similar cogent reason. This is an emerging pattern which should surely be taken by Teresa May as a warning. The Inquiry is seen by those most likely to benefit from it, victims of abuse and professionals trying to help them, as a cover-up of cover-ups. It has been set up because the establishment is no longer trusted by those most vulnerable to the abuse of power. No wonder there is now a power struggle being waged over its composition, remit and structure.

At the heart of the choices made about who is to chair the Inquiry and who is to sit on the panel are some fundamental questions. Who is to decide the process? Who is to control it? Who can be relied on to speak truth to power? The main group of stakeholders are surely those survivors who have been abused then betrayed again via inaction and the concealment of evidence and are now not assured of a process in which they can take part. They have been patronised as a 'victim community' by Woolf and as yet have no structured way of giving evidence.

Professionals and survivors witnessing and working in the field of child protection for decades have collective experience that should be helpful and is being overlooked. We wish to know why. Is it part of the continuing need for containment and denial that acknowledged experts in the field who have thought and learned most about the problems are not being consulted? Some are labelled as beyond the pale in terms of the establishment; some have had their careers constrained and blighted by the need of society not to know the truth about these things. Yet this group has hung on in there hoping one day that society will begin to acknowledge the enormous iceberg of systemic abuse in our midst and will want to know what they can tell them about its deliberate containment and use of scapegoating to deflect public concern.

This is a big ask, of course. But the questions for today might be, how can the evidence of survivors be heard and acted on? What alternatives are there to an inquiry which inspires no confidence? For example, why is the whole issue not being given the status and resources of a Royal Commission? This of course would be extremely costly, it would not be a quick fix, but would perhaps be a fitting acknowledgement by government and society of the extent of the institutional cover-ups from the 1980s and even earlier decades. It might go some way to restoring the faith of those who most need the truth to emerge.
Sue Richardson, Psychotherapist
Heather Bacon, Consultant Clinical Psychologist (retired)

*

Ex-Labour leader Ed Miliband made a statement, saying that the government should get a move on in setting up a national inquiry into organised child abuse. "The case now is overwhelming for the Government to get an overarching inquiry into child abuse up and running. We have seen scandals of child abuse in different institutions, in different parts of the country and stretching across different decades. An overarching inquiry has been delayed too long and needs to get moving as fast as possible to start listening to all those who have been let down by a system set up to protect them." (BBC News)

This is in sharp contrast to the condescending and evasive reply that Ed Miliband's office gave to a handwritten letter from Peter McKelvie demanding a national inquiry, which referred to an open letter to David Cameron (see below). The reply sounds like it's discussing a complaint about roadworks, instead of decades of horrific child abuse and subsequent cover-ups by people in authority.

Miliband's main interest in supporting an inquiry at this late stage seems to be political expediency, after Labour-run Rotherham council has been shown to have allowed fourteen-hundred vulnerable children to have been abused, raped, and exploited over a sixteen-year period.

Chapter Nine

After all you've now read, do you understand why this book had to be written and published?

There's so much I still haven't said and which you still don't know. You may remember mentions of the abuse or the inquiry on local news a few years ago, but they didn't show the facts. These were put into a report and no one knew what really happened unless they were in care themselves.

I didn't even know about the report; someone I know in authority gave me the link to it, saying, "Use this if you need to."

You can look for yourself. Visit https://spotlightonabuse.wordpress.com/ and see for yourself what the government think they found. They've missed out loads of boys and abusers.

The boys and girls I met in care are my brothers and sisters. They always will be. I've written this book for them and the lost ones who aren't here today.

I hope the ones that are still with us have made something of their life, despite what happened to them. All I can say is this, "Chin up and keep fighting. I know it's hard and we are in pain, but take each day as it comes, like I do. We got past that abuse. That means something, it means we're fighters. There is light at the end of the tunnel for all of us, just keep going. I'm doing this for each and every one of you that got through it. I know you're in pain, that you may suffer darkness…sleepless nights…anger and hate. The contempt we hold for our abusers will never go, we've just got to learn to cope with it—on our own and in our own way."

I know how it feels to think no fucker cares. I know how to put a fake smile on my face and how to insist to friends that I'm fine. Deep down, I'm dead. My soul has gone. The abusers took it from me at a young age.

To then be called a liar when I did speak up, no wonder I ran away so often. Every kid that ran off did so for the same reason: he was getting picked on, beaten up…maybe he was even sexually abused.

No fucker wanted to know. They just caught us and took us right back into their hands…to be slapped, kicked, punched, starved, and locked in a dark room with no clothes on for days on end. What sort of people do that to young kids? There's no name for sick bastards like this. Ask yourself why so many of us ended up in jail and in trouble with the police at such a young age. There's your answer: it's down to those wankers. They made us this way.

Some of the abused were able to snap out of it, lead a normal life and get jobs, but the weaker ones—who can't sleep at night or go out; the ones that were robbed of their families— they're on their own. They're the ones that need the most help, but they don't get it. They just get put on the sick for the rest of their life and told they will never work. How wrong is that?

Benefits are even lower than the basic wage. It's fucking wrong. You're abused as a child, then you're abused again years down the line.

We're told that we have problems. Yes, and who gave us those problems? The fucking abusers.

They might be dead now, but I'm not. I've just to cope on benefits for the rest of my life. Lives wrecked and we're just left alone to get on with it.

Why did the government close the inquiry? Did it cost too much to fund? Why is there not more support out there for abused care leavers? Not once have I ever had help with housing funding, despite being in care from the age of eight.

It's like you lose your real life to your abuser and you're just left in limbo as the days pass. If you're reading this and can identify with my dark past, know that you're not on your own. It's like I still have the abusers inside my head, telling me to say nothing, slowly killing my life off. The voices tell me I'm worthless, but I've never listened to them. I'm a fighter, and so are you…don't let that fucking abuser win. Shine like a star, my friend, and live that happy life. You deserve to.

I've worked hard to put this book together and I've suffered for years and years. It's about time I did something about the abuse, and if that means putting my life on paper then so be it.

I don't trust doctors and I hate therapy. What I went through isn't the plot of a movie. Therapists get paid to listen; I'll walk home feeling worse than I did before I arrived. No, thank you, I've dealt with my illness for twenty years without help or medication.

I didn't know if I was coming or going, living or dying, then I found the internet. That helped me a lot, talking to people who would never meet me from the other side of the world. There was always someone there when I wanted them.

Doctors just want to pump you full of tablets. Tablets make you worse. Reading this, you may think I need to see a doctor. Been there, done that. "Nothing wrong with you," they'd say, "just take these tablets for six weeks, you'll feel fine."

"Yeah, like fuck." I did try them once and, fucking hell, I felt like shit! I was so low, and I had a face like a wet lettuce. I haven't taken anything since.

There's nothing that tablets can do, I've just got to face facts and get on with things. They're not going to be able to eradicate my past life, are they? I wish they could; I even asked the doctor this. He said no, nothing like that exists. Maybe I'll feel better when this book is published and out there. When I don't have to hide away. Maybe I'll continue to feel like shit for the rest of my life—who knows? I know one thing: IT WAS NOT MY FAULT. I tell myself that every day and will do until the day I die.

I have lost my kids, my friends, even my mother over all this. I have a wonderful girlfriend now and a stepfamily that I love; I had to say goodbye to my real family years ago. That doesn't bother me now, things happen. I went into care as a young, innocent boy. When I came out, I'd changed—I wasn't that little boy anymore. I was full of hate…I still am. I still feel anger towards my mother. I do hate her, and she knows why. She won't face me to talk about the things she did, when she just left me there.

She knew I was being beaten up, I cried my fucking eyes out on the phone to her and begged to come home. And she put the phone down on me more than once. How can a mother do that to her son? Her fucking blood? I'd not done anything to her as a child. Okay, when I came out of those dark places I got into trouble and did silly things, most lads do who come out of care homes and prison—but not once did she ever come to any kids' home and try and get me out. I was dumped there, and she carried on, living a happy life.

There are people who cause drama for me or who won't talk to me to try and sort things out. I don't need those people in my life, though I wish them well. And if I've ever done anyone wrong, I'm sorry for my behaviour—that's to family members and anyone else who thinks I was a little dickhead as a young kid. I've grown up now and I'm happy. I hope this book shows that everyone can change.

I've had this book in my head for twenty-five years. It feels great to offload, but I'm really doing this so that others don't choose the path I did. You don't want to end up like me. I never listened to anyone, and I still don't. I am who I am, and if anyone doesn't agree with what I've written, stop reading now and put this book down; it's not for you, but have a happy life.

Over the last eight years I've not had so much as a parking fine, which is a huge turnaround from someone who was always in shit with the police. I know I've not always done good, but I don't believe I'm a bad person either. I'm not proud of my charge sheet or some of the things I've done, but I'm trying to make it up for it now.

I've stayed away from trouble and I'm now living a normal life in a nice house. I even have a driving licence; I'm legal. No drugs, no crime. I'm settled and I'm happy, it just took me a long time to realise my mistakes.

No one's perfect, though some like to make out they are. Sorry to be crude, but everyone's shit stinks. People like that, in my experience, turn out to be bullies.

Now the internet is here, and I have the help I need, I knew I could make public the abuse that goes on. I can show how hard it's been and that I've finally managed to get past it all. It's not being easy…in fact, it's been a fucking nightmare: fights, hospitals, bike crashes, car crashes, jails, police cells, drugs, drink; the darkness, sadness, loss of family and friends. I wish I'd done this years ago.

I've been seven stone through various breakdowns, stress and illnesses. I've also been fifteen stone—still ill, but better than I was. I don't think I'll ever get over my illness, but who would after the life I've had to deal with? I knew people who ended up taking their lives. Lads who hung themselves, people that cut their wrists. It's sad, so fucking sad. I give my full respect to those who have taken their lives because of the abuse. It took me a long time, but I finally managed to pull myself away from the drugs, the evil, the horrors. I've come out the other side happy.

My girlfriend got me to go out for the day; it took her two weeks to get me out that day. If it hadn't been for her I would never have seen a better side of myself. I can't thank her enough.

Chapter Ten

Lancaster Farms' prison was new when I was there. I was the sixty-third inmate. It was great, like a youth club. Everything was new: the cells, the flooring, the doors, the phones; it was like a hotel but with locked doors and screws that locked you up twice a day, at night and in the afternoon. They'd let you out again, unless you were banged up for being a little dickhead like me. I gave them shit on a daily basis.

Here, you had things to do, like cooking, gym, cleaning, art and computers. If you didn't wish to do any of these things you could stay in bed and do fuck all with your time.

I was only there for twenty-eight days, so it really was a piece of piss for me; however, other lads had two years…three years…and more.

The new jail was always going to have lads there, and I figured that it wouldn't be long until it was full.

I met all sorts in there, all my age. We'd talk about our crimes—some petty, some bigger…there were even bank robbers in with us. And there was me, sitting there on a charge of robbing a car, thinking I was Billy Big Spuds. I'd only just turned sixteen.

I'd listen to the older lads as they told their stories—it was fucking great. You didn't butt in, though, or you might cop a punch; that's how it was.

I'd read the reports they had to do for court. The lads from Toxteth were all sound. One was as hard as fuck; he had this saying, "If you don't have a one-time punch then sit in your cell." (A one-time punch is where you knock lads out with one punch.)

*

Stoke Heath: this place was a fucking dump—and I mean, a fucking dump. It had no toilets; you had a piss-pot, like a bucket. What a fucking nightmare. You did your thing in the pot then you'd have to take it to the wash-house—it was called slopping out. The screws would open your door and shout, "Slop out, lads!"

It was sick. I've seen more shit flying than birds in the sky. You'd try and get up quickly to sort your shit bucket out, so that you could get back in your cell before you got in the way of some lad's bucket going over a screw's head. It was that bad, though sometimes it was funny to see a big, fat screw covered in shit.

This happened every day, and the gym was where it all went off. There were Scousers and Mancs—we hated them all, but there'd be too much going on with their own gang wars for them to bother with us. There were also lads from Moss Side, Wythenshawe and Salford, as it was a Manchester jail. There were still some hard fuckers in there from Liverpool, as well as the twins from Kirby and the twins from Birkenhead who knocked lads out for fun. It was one big boxing ring.

The screws would open your cell door and lads would just run in and twat you for being a Scouser, even if you came from the Wirral. The screws were all pricks…evil bastards; they didn't care if you lived or died. I saw lads carried out who had hung themselves.

I was released with no bones broken, thank fuck. I vowed that I would never go back there. We all said that…and did we come back? Yes, time and time again. It's still the same today: dark, evil and full of horrors.

Pulling up at my new prison, I was lucky: there was a load of Scousers as well as the twins from Kirby on my bus, so I felt relatively safe. I was only there for four months, but that was a long time in that shithole. I came there from my first sentence knowing nothing about car crimes, drugs, bank robbers, killers, and even sick kiddie fiddlers. I was only there on a shitty burglary charge.

I walked into the main reception and into a holding cage that held twenty lads, all from Liverpool, who had been kicked out of the Farms. We got past there and onto the main wings; it was dark and stank of piss.

"Follow me, cunts," this shithead screw shouted.

He was a big shithead and one of the twins shouted, "Fuck off, knobhead."

"This is it," I thought, "we're all going to get twatted now."

Thankfully, the screw just said, "I'll get you after, Scouse cunt."

It was the same routine as all the other prisons, only here you would be banged up 24/7, in your cell for twenty-four hours a day. If you were lucky, you'd get a shower once a week.

The screws hated us Scousers and we all knew it. The food was nasty: green custard, like bright green mushy peas. If you didn't eat it, you'd starve, so you had to eat their shit food and just get on with it.

Most of the fights were down in the gym…some would even kick off in the chapel! We'd all have to back each other up when the Manchester lot wanted to fight; there was no backing out, otherwise you'd be done in by your own boys.

If you were shipped out with other lads, you knew to stick together in the next place. The following prison was miles away and I was on my own—there weren't many Scousers there, but I got on with everyone. It was a massive jail, relatively new…full of black lads, and white lads who thought they were black (lads from Birmingham and Wolverhampton).

London gangs fought Birmingham gangs. Wolverhampton gangs fought other gangs. It was fucking mad. Still the same routine, only a much bigger jail and more lads, more screws, bigger sentences. There'd be gang wars with the burger bar boys, they were all in for gun crimes and drugs. They'd clash and smash the prison up. I saw one riot in my time, and it was bad; gates were ripped off the hallways, screws were beaten up and inmates ran the wings with drugs. Eventually, more screws came, and it was all shut down. The cells were on fire, the wings were on fire, lads were getting beaten up by the riot screws…the whole place kicked off on shut down.

It was in the newspapers: prison riots in Wolverhampton Prison.

I got eighteen months, so I was shipped around other prisons on the one sentence. It felt like a long sentence from jail to jail—I even spent time down the block, away from other prisoners.

People talk of getting raped in prison. That's a load of shit. People who say that have never even been in one. Not once in all my prison days did I see or hear anything about anyone being sexually abused.

*

HM Prison Deerbolt is a male juveniles' prison and Young Offenders Institution located in the village of Startforth, in County Durham, England. That place was a fucking shit tip. It had plastic in the windows and it was fucking cold. All the inmates hated lads from Merseyside; when I was put in here young Jamie Bulger was sadly murdered, so the local lads hated any of us for what those two evil bastards did to that poor boy.

Eventually, things settled down in there. It went from nasty shouts to, "Alright, Scouse?" The place was massive: fifteen wings, fifteen units, five landings high and I was right at the fucking top. Cell fourteen, cold as fuck. It was in here that I got my first beating from the screws. I was pulled down to the block and beaten up. I was given black eyes, the lot…kicked, punched, stripped, then locked in this other cell for seven days.

In all my days of prison life I never received one letter or visit. It sounds shocking, but I just got on with it.

I was moved on again to Glen Parva. That was a massive place as well. I got my red band in there, which meant I could walk around the prison and deal with the others. Inmates were roughly sixteen to twenty, and came from everywhere: Wales, London, Liverpool, Manchester, Birmingham, Wolverhampton, Scotland, even Ireland. The working classes did as they were told; I did industrial cleaning jobs to make the days go faster. Some lads just stayed in their cells.

It was a clean place, really. I was there for a good few months and it was my last stint in Young Offenders.

*

My next prison sentence saw me sent to an adult prison: Altcourse. My first big man's jail, as they say. It was like an open prison within a prison. You had key fobs to get around the place.

It was full of wrong 'uns as well. By 'wrong 'uns' I mean abusers, kiddie fiddlers. They walked around as freely as everyone else. You could wear your own clothes and jewellery and there were even TVs and snooker tables.

Lads would run around with their jackets on back to front; they'd run in your cell and rob your canteen (if you were a muppet). I saw legs, arms and jaws snapped in there. The lads ran the prison from when it was first opened—they just overtook the screws.

The screws called you by your first name. You'd have to go to work and do what you were told, otherwise you'd be banged up with no wages. I chose the CD workshop.

I was there for three months, released in 1995. I managed to stay out of prison for four years then I picked up some daft charges.

In 1999 I was sent to Walton. The Big House, they call it in Liverpool. Sefton Magistrates sent me there in a 'sweat box'—the tiny metal cages inside the 'meat van', which you're forced to sit in all the way to your destination.

I was here just before Christmas that year. It kicked off big time. My first time in the yard and there was a fucking riot over tobacco and food.

The prison was smelly and it was falling down. The screws had their own law: they'd beat up lads and throw inmates' mail in the bin. They were told they were not allowed visitors and their families were turned away from the place.

That was my last port of call in such an institution. My jail time stopped there.

*

The story today….

As I write this, I'm as shocked and horrified to remember the details as I was to experience them first-hand.

It's been a cathartic process, but nothing will ever make me forget.

My time and focus now is spent helping survivors of abuse in the care system. I organise local boxing matches, donating all proceeds to various children's homes and organisations, alongside other charity work.

I continue to fight to see my abusers pay for their crimes. And I continue to give a voice to those who have been abused where no one has listened.

Fight Your Fears

Grove House

Saint Vincent's

Red Bank

Bryn Melyn

My first flat, twelth floor

Me

Stoke Heath

Hindley Young Offenders' Institution

Deerbolt Young Offenders' Institution

Altcourse

Walton

My best mate, Stephen Quirk

Betty Thomas, always looked out for me.

Printed in Great Britain
by Amazon